W9-BLL-700

Armed Love

13.10

ARMED
LOVE

by

Eleanor Lerman

Wesleyan University Press
Middletown, Connecticut

Copyright © 1973 by Eleanor Lerman

Library of Congress Cataloging in Publication Data
Lerman, Eleanor, 1952-
    Armed love.

    (The Wesleyan poetry program, v. 68)
    Poems.
    I. Title.
PS3562.E67A9   811.5'4   73-6013
ISBN 0-8195-2068-3
ISBN 0-8195-1068-8 (pbk.)

Manufactured in the United States of America
First edition

PS
3562
.E67
A9

For the Harpsichordettes

Contents

Armed Love

The Quality of the Film

I am not nearly as pleased with myself as I am
with the quality of the film
A week before the cameras and her first line is
Sweetie, which one of us do you suspect is
morally perverse?
In my own time I contemplate: warm water baths are tried
and salted wine
I do exercises for cramped legs, and wandering in the
Great Auditorium I find the marble proscenium has been
    disfigured
with obscene words therefore
the house is rearranged
the necessity for spotlights is discussed and clothes
sewn shut or ripped apart
A month before the cameras and still I am
only making gestures
The weather, of course, has not been with me (this will
sound good in conversation) and she refuses to wear anything
that is not a true gift
Still, I would not be making films if it were simple
Ten years before the cameras and her next line is
Sugar, which one of us do you suspect
has never been ashamed?
Frances, in a moment you will understand   there you are
dancing naked in your wig and
even sitting on the bathroom floor
I could go on writing love poems for days

Margaret Whiting Tearfully Sings

Then there were those days on lower Broadway
using just enough to keep a room at the
University Hotel so you could sit at the window
in your lime green underwear hoping for some business
or at least a pure shot
for old times sake
all I could do
was sit on the toilet and drool into a paper cup
asking you to drink milk
to go to sleep to
please
get dressed or get undressed completely
Instead
you brought the radio into the bathroom
touching my hair while I cried over Margaret Whiting singing
'Moonlight in Vermont'   one more time one more
time

where are you
where are all your friends whose taste ran to
imitation red leather and see through blouses that kept me
weeping on the toilet for days on end
I still worry about the people I didn't make love to
were their grandmothers ever cured, did they
earn enough money
did someone find them in time

The Basic Cruelties of Life in New York City

There are too many women in this city
who have to sit out traffic jams
because they are too fat to squeeze between
the bumpers of trucks and taxis
These are the same women
who live in ground floor apartments
with windows that open onto the street
arranged with gold fringed american flags,
plastic flowers, and no husband

There are too many clerical positions (lt. type
40 wpm, div. dut.) open in this city
for small, neatly groomed girls
with lacquered fingertips
and tiny diamonds on their left hands
These are the same girls who will put on
iridescent pink dresses
and show up occasionally at the club on Mott Street
where the police are invited in for drinks and cash
but no dancing

There are too many people
that you can find on East Houston Street tonight
who are sexually confused
trying to eat as much cocaine as possible
before being murdered for the package
These are the same people you find
consorting with clerks in iridescent dresses
slipping like poisoned shadows ($5.00 a bag
$10.00 a bag) through midtown traffic jams

Celebration

The morning after I leave my job
I will make up with the bitch queen and
return to Spring Street involved with the orange juice and
narcotics diet
The people I work for will replace me and my
neighbors will stop being so polite
when they realize how I'm paying the rent
however
the greatest non-union shoplifting
team in New York City will be
back in business and although
this may not actually be a fit subject
for a poem
when it is four o'clock in the
morning and you have just decided to give up
typing and clean living forever
some sort of celebration is called for

The Mental Hermaphrodite Dreams a Better Cake

The candy bride my mother kept for me
in a blue tray with all those bangly earrings
melted in despair one summer as if
the confusion of bathrooms, the expensive
medications stolen into the
wrong hands and all those handsome vampires
who left here with kiss scarred fangs and
blue trays full of fancy cosmetics
had proved to her that her services were
obsolete if not actually tragic

the pink and white puddle I
wrapped in wax
ed paper and returned to the candy factory
in New Jersey with a note read
ing   Please send something less
sensitive
I am a mental hermaphrodite awash
in a wedding cake of chemical dreams

Enchantment in a Jar

Thoughtfully, the last queen telephones
from the barren kingdom revealing
that all the silver bibles have been sold
for pharmaceuticals and large jars of vaseline
Because I need these things for my body we make
an arrangement: I can have the first night
and all the white powders if, when she decides to go off
and do enchanted things with the contents of
the medicine cabinet
I will watch the Sword of the Spirit which,
she confides in me
is only made of fool's gold

Graduate School

Time after time the
hygiene instructor warned us
about inserting things in
embarassing places, having fatal accidents
unless accompanied by a duly certified
red cross monitor, and of course
there were those delicate shudders and
intimations about crossing
sexual lines   (you know)

this is to inform you
ladies that the courses they teach
out here in the free world
are more frequently attended and I don't think
that if all the wonderful
people I've brought home from
class so far
got together in one place we could
isolate one single, clear
sexual line even if we
stayed up all night and whistled
dixie

One of the nights I do not kill myself
I count eleven roaches in the cornflakes
and decide not to tell anybody
also one irregular star nicely framed
between the scratches on the window
Smoking unfiltered cigarettes in the kitchen
I study the plans pasted on all four walls
hoping they are for a nuclear reactor
to be built secretly inside the Women's
House of Detention
or for a computerized whore house
I can visit as a special guest
(I know the owner, I know the designer of the plans)
Nicol doesn't tell us what these drawings
meticulously measured and scaled with a T-square
are to be used for
little noises come from the bedroom where the boys are
little whispers from the hall
I go on to smoke all the Turkish cigarettes because
I do not expect Nicol home until morning
with the money to buy orange juice
the money for roach spray
I prevent my suicide
by reciting the names written on the bedroom wall
Marianne & Barbara
Marianne & Cathy
John & Steven & Lee
my name is next to the metal wardrobe
although I wrote it myself and drew a box around it
causing a lot of trouble with Marianne
There are a few moments when I still think of
getting a job, behaving in a better fashion

but John tells me (as I comb his hair
as I help him dress) that suicides
must be always protected by their friends
and constantly kept occupied
I have memorized the wall
I am counting roaches
little noises come from the bedroom
little whispers from the hall

Your other girlfriends ate all the cereal last night
you'll have to go out in the rain and find a grocery
that's open Sunday mornings
perhaps bring back some aspirin
I'm going to be bleeding in the sink all afternoon
and I need my nourishment
this should not worry you as long as I am able
to entertain your old friends and
take you dancing one night a week
Turn on the radio before you go
I want some fancy music to cheer up the water bugs
they may let me use the shower
if they're feeling good
The bathroom mirror your brother broke
is showing me hundreds of faces
that are all mine
bloodless, torn, unslept in
If I believed you hated me as much as you
sometimes think you do
I would swear you had done this to my face
as a personal statement
Bring back some sugar coated cereal
with free offers on the boxtops
there are a lot of things I need that no one gives me

I Will Find You Old Families

All that you wanted will be granted to you
the French name that you lie about, here
I give it to you
call yourself what you will
swear you are the daughter of fallen nobility
I will find old families for you to visit
I will encourage you
Money in a Swiss bank, here,
here are the forged papers, the soft leather checkbooks
the stolen credit letters
pretend you were born in Normandy and your
grandmother adores you, the grandmother
with the jewels that belonged to an empress
swear you are the child of an empress
I will believe you
Ask for anything; white skin, black hair
I give you beauty, I give you grace, I give you
eternal youth
Half of my life, here,
here is half of my life
love me, abandon me
its useless, it doesn't matter
I will swear I am a Saxon king, a Greek prince
in exile, a true alchemist
Blood, swords, cruelty, glory
all this is yours, all this I grant you
it's useless, it doesn't matter

The Cooking Utensils Can, I Think, Be Left at Home

I realize that you always wanted scented
bathroom powders and French maids to
stroke your ankles
Somebody must have sold you all the
wrong books; you're expecting me to offer
my arm and take you for long walks
around Central Park
perhaps buy you little pieces of jewelry and
anniversary gifts
I can see you are planning to serve me
elaborate casseroles when I come home
and occasionally call me at work and giggle (sweetly)
Somebody brought you up all wrong

glass bottles baby
are going to get strewn in your path
and we're going to be spending a lot of time
in empty apartments
sleeping in illegal positions
I'll show you the profitable parts of Central Park
you'll learn to love it

The Graceless Years

The years of the scientists begin

I realize that it is useless to plead insanity
this is what they expect
carefully I unbutton my collar exposing
the bite marks, the rows of scars
if I am bleeding now, no one tells me

some small remark on my part interests them
in my wrists
they are not astonished to see the line
from my middle finger runs down
into my arm
consequently, they take my papers from me
perhaps they change my fingerprints

I dream at night of climbing
cold, wet walls
I find salamanders with deep green eyes whispering
herb cures in my ear
my pulse is checked, my eye movements noted
I dream that my neck is healed
this terrifies me

I know my case is not unique
sometimes I hear other voices in the corridor
a finger is left lying carelessly on the floor
possibly they are deciding if I should be
returned to my family, or if I would be more useful
under controlled conditions
they give me medicine
I overhear one surgeon say that they should operate

close the latest wound I have inflicted
someone else feels this is unnecessary

unfortunately, I have kept the golden needles with me
all this time
I have a terrible, screaming dream (jewelled frogs,
bandages) and a nurse discovers them on me
as she tries to administer a sedative
they fall to the floor
and she is almost blinded
a conference is held
my family will have to pay for the nurse's convalescence
my needles are destroyed
the scientists are triumphant
they have found out
how I tear my throat, why my lines are ill formed
I am told my throat will heal now
horror, horror

on the eighth night I make love to a bacteriologist's wife
while she is thrashing on the bed I steal one of her hair clips
with a sharp clasp
finally she falls asleep and I escape
through her bedroom window
I am beginning to feel more relaxed now, more hopeful
as I attack my throat I notice this is an
expensive neighborhood of tall apartment buildings
if you look up you can see half a constellation
one tenth the arc of a starship pulling for Venus
the blood feels very warm on my fingers, very good

somewhere above me a group of nuclear scientists
are having a party on an enclosed roof garden and I know

o I know

that before morning
they'll all be falling into the street

Prison as a Place of Worship

By the time they realized
that they should never have put us in the same cell
I had revealed the translation of the Martian obelisk
and promised you the crushed disc of star-mined silver
sewn into my palm
Cloistered in my theoretical wingspan
you wrote a letter to the warden saying
I have changed my mind. A medical examination
will prove nothing
When the matrons arrived
it was a hundred years too late
The iron shadow of the starship
had already grown old and impatient
above the spinning earth

The Alchemist Lost to Human Gifts

While I am yet trembling with the need to give you gold
you are shutting up my workshop.
giving away the lead pipes I have hoarded for a century
Gently you take my books from me
professing to love more my human gifts of sulphur and salt
When I cry out in my sleep
still tempted by immortality
you press the white rose, the red rose into my hands
and talk to me
mentioning the names of those you know
still sleepwalking between Illium and mighty Greece

Not Least of All the Horn

Someone knows

I have always been careful that my make-up
should conceal the horn
and every precaution has been taken
against my being seen at meals
in the basement of the house
yet, I begin to feel that someone is remembering

suddenly, the servants are gone
someone has told them a story about a forced labor in 1842
I am alone with all these crippled animals to care for

I wake one morning with an eagle's breath
on my face
to find my house is full of deranged birds
each bird has a silver band around its neck
I know what words are written there
Wandering all morning in my robe I find
passages and long marble halls
I never saw before
there seems to be an old ballroom, a dusty
tower bedroom with fruitwood chairs that are
difficult to sit in
in each room there are small piles of burning books
I know which books

now, even my gardens cannot calm me
I sit amidst the cyclamen pouring acid
over the marks cut into my palm
but I know there are other proofs

someone is beginning to understand
someone has been told about my mother's premonitions

then of course there are the letters
the rumors about those letters

GARDNER WEBB COLLEGE LIBRARY

Tarot

As we entered into the summer solstice I felt
for the first time that I need not consult the oracle
I carried you down to the boiling sea and alone,
constructed the proper ritual
When you were able to join unaided in my difficult recitation
I let you bathe for hours in the sand that I had already turned
to particles of light
When the storm broke

you had my oldest gift, and at last I heard you say
so you've always been the devil
For a time you considered your new position
while I gathered broken souls washing up on the shore.
When you came to help me I understood
this would be a marriage of unusual duration.
Worldly longing we gathered into coffee cans
with burning sand and tiny souls
and with all hope of paradise we started home
sorting and repairing the first few to be reborn.
As our neighbors now

pass by our glowing door
they kindly touch their children's eyes and say
therein dwells the devil and his wife
she of the lightning, the incredible silver hands.

Armed Love

Were you making films with me when you wore your white
    shirts
the way Brando wore white shirts?
All week at the Olympia I have been watching him
in his BEST FILMS tense
with armed love, terrifying the audience with the one true
feeling, hardly diminished by the bad prints
These nights, they run movies in my mind: a man
in a witch's hat tells me
that vampires are happier when they're homosexual
and while this may or may not be true
It was one of my BEST FILMS and probably
took years of working up to
At intermission they show a message: a man
in an evening dress grins and points to
his sign: all love is armed and shown
only on screen
He has your face
Sweetheart come back to me
I begin to see your throat so sweet
for lips or teeth
the half kiss, the kiss goodnight
Pay your director and let him go
I will show you how I've learned to handle a camera
I have movie theatres in my eyes
a library of classic films for you
to take advantage of

Alone, the Actor and His Child Embrace

Alone, the once great american movie actor
and his child embrace
In her eyes he sees crazy Indians he had to kill
and all the women he didn't get to make love to on screen
because they knew he meant it
Together, they go to film festivals to see
the pictures he made when he was young and enigmatic
Beneath the white ray of the movie projector he grows
fat and ungraceful, while his daughter watches his
beautiful screen face
understanding the great american terror he carried
so long against his skin, the rippling
bloody hero who occasionally put his hand
to his head in some gentle movement that was always
edited out
She courts the women she hates
who touch their blonde hands to her difficult face
expecting the actor's young flesh to rise up
out of her body and perform violent,
Indian killing acts of love
She does
and goes home to reward her father for his gestures of kindness
for each learned act of unamerican mercy
Alone, he brings her into his arms
knowing she will become crazy and remain inside
with a loaded shotgun
He will grow old and die a woman
knowing that what passes for love is behind everything

Rockaway, approx. 1969

I couldn't explain to you then why men seem to
come and go as they please because I was
too concerned with public opinion to be truthful
There was a story I used to tell
about the young, homosexual daughter
of a famous american movie star
who coerced a whole high school full of boys
into singing counter-tenor on a New York radio station
It was a lie
Only men make money

Wasn't I good though, screaming in my fake falsetto
while I laced up your boots
'Yoo hoo girlie. Don't appear to be selling anything.
We never did get much local cooperation

I also lied about the bleach in the bathwater
and about where I got the meals
but I'm here now
I'm not as well as I used to be, but I am here
There aren't very many other possibilities
I'm running out of food, clothing,
employment opportunities and narcotics

I have in my possession a silver brain I bought
by stealing coupons from every supermarket
I worked in
Looking at it kept me calm in the evenings on that icy peninsula
when I had to be so careful of keeping my hands
away from your face
because the commercial values of out-of-season resorts
always take into consideration the use

and texture of exposed skin
I was going to buy our freedom from north america
with meat coupons
and I'm sorry I didn't tell you about it first

Very simply, I am inaugurating eternity
and ending all terrorist relationships
that I thought had style
but don't go
I'm not planning the usual progress of events
after a remarriage
This time I expect to stay alive,
just to be near you

Shotgun Days

Get out the pistol honey
and warn me about eating all those silver
bullets because one
blue blue morning
suicide and money won't be enough
sexual pain won't be enough not all the
fancy cowgirls learning to trick the
trade not all the breakfast cereals from here to
Checkerboard Farms will be enough to calm me
down   Get out the pistol baby
and arm the neighbors because one
blue blue morning
I'll have strange notions about the bedclothes
a desperate fear about some Spanish woman
about the killing taste inside my tongue
Get down slowly off the table and warn me
about a pearl's weight against your shoulder
iron's pure color against your cheek

she steps out of her nightgown and will not let me
sleep as someone moans o god
its going to be one of those shotgun
days

Finally I See Your Skin

Finally I see your skin so scarred
by my use that I can close my eyes and tell you
where the constant embrace of my fingers is turned to gold
on your stomach, and the press of my legs
has turned your thighs to polished glass
No one else thinks of touching you now
Your body mentions me in all its movements
and has come to fit only into my hands

I once told you that I had celestial information
cut on the insides of my mouth and it was years
before you wore it smooth enough to keep from
bleeding your tongue
Mindful of this
you come to kiss me one morning and find
I am old and brittle and pure
my mouth cracks open and planets start to pour out
universes form and begin to show
signs of life

In Your Movements I See Drownings

I think I used to live by an ocean somewhere
but I don't remember much more
There was a school, a movie house, maybe a friend
I must have had just a friend once
maybe she drove a car, maybe that's where I started
constructing your appearance
in a small car trapped on a highway with everything
getting blurry and too much music
maybe I thought you worked in a store someplace
and said to my friend *stop here*
I have to go into that store
or you were dancing in a bar, or being sick
on the floor of a hospital
I can't remember
I don't want you to remember
I won't mention you to fate anymore, and I don't want
to go outside
Just to remain here and discuss you with myself
establish just why I see terrible things happening when
    you move
this will be a life's work, an affair
of great durability, concern, many written pages
It is impossible for me to walk down stairs anymore
because the people walking up look into my face
as if we had danced together once in a great, empty hall,
as if they want to say something
and I see you killing them
bringing back to me their personal jewellry, the photographs
in their wallets
knowing that I really wanted these things done for me
or wanted to do them for you
I want to steal personal histories and private lives and

scatter them across your pillow to prove that really
we're the only ones alive
I understand that your cruelty is necessary to me
I sleep curled closely against your cruelty
absorbing it, honoring myself with it
pleased that I am a person cruelties are done for
Nobody can talk like me
that is all I want you to remember
say it to yourself when you're apart from me so you know
where I am, what I'm doing
I will be listening for your footsteps
waiting to see civilizations drowning in the movements
    of your hands
cities raped and plundered in the air around your head

I Will Teach You About Murder

I want you to know that for you
I am going to occasionally destroy
large cities with fire and earthquakes and
murder great numbers of helpless people because
if you keep looking at me like that
night after night
for the next few thousand years
I am going to keep you locked in my arms
teaching you where madness touches love

A Personal History

Even when you were a schoolgirl
curled up on my sofa with your Trojan histories
I was studying a more educated cruelty,
comparing our blood types for the hereditary inclination
that would later defeat all reasonable arguments
I know you didn't expect me to play tennis with you
or politely entertain your relatives
but when I had you
for the first time waiting in my arms
did you have to so calmly throw back your head and say
I understand
this is to be a personal annihilation

Bell and I

We were raised in an institution for the impaired
Bell and I, and took an early fancy
to each other's diagnostic charts
I always brought the drugs for her tea
and she was considerate enough to keep
the pictures I took with my camera eyes,
this supposedly being one of my difficulties
It bothered me little, however, that I was partially invisible
because it gave me greater mobility
but I had to keep it from the Head that my body
was as yet unopened
This was the basis of his therapy:
open the body and rearrange!
Investigate! Seek out the impairment!
Cures were common, but dull

When I was fourteen the city supervisor came round
and put me in a welfare film about arrested heredity
Being one of the last remaining mental orphans
I became a big star, appearing in many documentaries
about malfunctioning body systems
(I can still do all the poses)
and got Bell out of the home after I was officially paroled
I set her up in a fancy card shop uptown
where she ran around in feathers and made lots of money
I couldn't get her to take off her clothes though, ever
After a while, she wouldn't even talk about the final diagnosis

When I was seventeen I had a daughter
and put her immediately into the institution
I felt bad about it of course, but she was a good girl
and managed to get me a letter now and then

41

The Head was still running the place, and was so pleased
to have another mental orphan
that he added a whole new wing
naming it The Memorial to Arbitrary Life
One day I got a telegram from my daughter
saying that she'd met some interesting people
from the third floor
during the breathing in the solarium
and would I come over and talk with them?
I did, and after just one conversation I knew
we'd all stepped out of the dream together,
a very long time ago

So I rang up Bell and told her to meet me
at my hotel/motel on the pike
Bell was only there a few minutes when my daughter walked in
having escaped the home by making herself partially invisible
She was crazy as a loon of course,
but all in all, still a good girl
I'd never told Bell I had a daughter, so for a while
it was a great reunion although I'm sure she didn't know
what the girl meant when she started saying
bye-bye sweet dreams!
bye-bye ladies of the culture!
I had to explain to Bell then
Bell, I said
she isn't really my daughter
Remember all those drugs I put in your tea?
All I meant really was that the girl was only
half as crazy as Bell, half as crazy as me
but poor Bell was so terrified she tried to get out of the room
We had to tie her up then with adhesive tape

We carried her to our campsite in the pines
and introduced her to my girl's friends
from the institution, who were Bell's parents,
both of them female, and younger than Bell
I was taking pictures of the event with my camera eyes
(which are no longer a difficulty)
but Bell got hysterical when we all ripped open our coats
to show her that our bodies were still unopened,
still unrearranged, still beautifully impaired
Bell, who was wearing three dresses,
a feather boa and a plaid cape refused to join us
or say anything further about the final diagnosis
I had meant all this as a kindness
but she wasn't having any of it
so we drove her back to town and gave her the line
about the way of all flesh etc. etc.

The last I heard Bell still refuses to believe
that we all made ourselves up
but she carries pine needles in her handbag
and hates women now, hates their faces

The girl in the red velvet trousers
was drinking bourbon with someone else's lemons when I
    walked in
She was well into that Last of the Great Lovers attitude:
lights around the eyes, chronometer watch, French cuffs,
and I've never forgotten it
I mean for her long hands and boyish face to become famous
but we'll have to shine up the surfaces around here
if we're going to make women popular
They have to be told about the back shadowed alcoves
the ones that Christmas bar lights don't seem to reach

How wrong can we be about love?
If you've got four dollars and a pink ticket
you can go promenading anywhere
but what makes that look so attractive is what I'm after
(not everyone gets to do a double image)
If you start acting sexy, the music gets turned up
and people start bumping into you
However, something does go on in those back rooms
Heads are left lying on tables, bodies go walking off together
and then the clothes just naturally match
That's what I want for my one night out with the ladies:
free movement, a respectable uniform
and a touching good-bye

I said how wrong can we be about love?
What shines should simply shine
and all the pink tickets lying on coat-room floors
should be given away
Watch.
Two people go off one night

and are later seen making private gestures
That's what we've got to know about:
the positioning, the look, the posture of the face

You say this is an all-purpose cleanser?
Hurry! Get me my wrist brace!
If we're going to get Casa Loco open
we have to keep the mystery mirrors gleaming
How personal our lives are going to be!

The Community of Women Causes an Operation

If you understood how much I need this
operation you would remove that revolver
from your hair and shoot your way out of
the women's museum
That's the story of my life doctor
the good girls I meet always show up wearing expensive
undergarments and John F. Kennedy Memorial Necklaces
You know, Jack, I used to be a woman until
I began suspecting these wet places on my body
of not remembering who they belong to
They can't simply belong to the community of women
If only someone could get me to a clinic
all the druggist does is rattle around in his bottles
and prescribe John F. Kennedy Memorial Vitamins
my god mr. president what's happened that we've both
come to this

What I've Got to Have, I've Got to Have

No wonder you're feeling so good-looking these days
Haven't I arranged to be a general of sorts
turned out in an elaborate jacket of black spangles
rattling a scented box of bones at the foot
of your wide bed, hinting
that god knows what may befall whoever's life you fancy
should be decorated by the sudden click
of the next roll?
Call up your friends
imply that life goes dancing on anyway
that a madwoman is sitting beside you
right now, writing military fashion letters
that arrive shining through the pockets of soldier ghosts
who stay and live in your closets on love alone
What will they say when we sneak up on them
at their offices and point out that the days
are beginning to glitter visibly
that the vibration of time is going to pierce the earth
and run it through so that nothing can prevent us
from accepting back into our taped-up limbs
whoever we used to be before those who lived
on the wing danced out and sanity came
slithering in?
Someone's got to teach these girls
that it all comes easy, that the boys won't tell
that love's all right if you do it right
and I think you're just the one to teach them
with your spangles on, with your homemade
hypnotizing drinks
I'll trust you with each life I'm going to have
if the costumes fit, and if the songs work out,
if you keep me drunk on lightning glass

poured into cups, into canisters, secreted
in my bureau drawer to light the days
you're away doing good works
for the sexually confused
They have their place, love, and you're just the one
to bend them right, and keep the social workers too busy
with the prettiest hoodlums to write reports
Dance me around a few more times
before the finest of all stories starts
and do something for me before I burn away
but it has to be the best of what you've got
because I'm becoming uncontrollable
flying around with your potent phonograph needle
recording the startled impulses of all those people
whose love I've got to have

Poem for Nefertiti

Crouching in the bedroom
surrounded by large dogs named King of Prussia
and breakfast dishes full of Cheerios and gin
I am sure that I can never write another poem
Terrified each morning
that some great sacrifice will be called for
I make plans to study typewriting
or to mail myself, finger by finger,
to the United States Government
Catching me with the silver shears and a dozen small boxes
you only break out a fresh package of wands
and repeat that your mother used to dream of Nefertiti
Subdued, I let you put the medicine in my eyes
and shut me up in my room
with reams of black paper
and one hundred multicolored pens

when each poem decides to kill me
I remind myself that I have a friend at home
who knows my fear of Egyptian sorcery
and I am helpless either way
Without my shears and typewriter
I need your merciful regulations
darling
you are my kindest prison

GARDNER WEBB COLLEGE LIBRARY

Officer, Even If I Am Jewish

What you want me to say is
that I am Jewish and I didn't have
anything to do with the
blonde girl locking herself
in the bathroom with the
small knife and the screaming
Officer, I was not trying to convert her

The Dream Cycle Begun Again

When the dream cycle begins again I cannot
offer you the protection of separate lives
having forgotten whose panic I am in
for I have passed you secretly in time and time again
to see myself curled inside your head and each step
you take becomes a cradle for my premonitions
each movement growing into me so that when I come to you
my mouth full of powders I cannot
eat or remove, it is your mouth sewn shut
by the adulteress wife of a dead king
Have so many years gone by that my body is
grown hollow and overflows with liquid gold
that I can love you only in some pure pain
that aches beyond you, beyond your
human comfort?
It is not without desire I kneel before you
having swallowed shards of glass you know are shards of moon
waiting for you to lean your head against my leg
and admit you are Antigone
promising a double death, a dream more wonderous
than disentangled grief

Perfect Together

The marriage took place in Northern Michigan
while nobody was looking
They exchanged 'meaningful glances' only
and spent some years ice-fishing on the lakes
The state police arrested them a few times but they
kept the cells full of tiny rocks, tossing them
back and forth between the bars
explaining that they were sending messages to each other
and the blonde kept pulling cold stars out of her eyes
that kept the temperature in the jail well
below freezing so the police finally drove them
to the Canadian border and told them to
stay out of trouble (leaving it all up to
the CRMP)
The darker one liked to sleep on the right side
to keep watch on the frozen mountains
but they took turns, because personal destiny
had little mention in their conversation anymore
Each time a season fell out of place
one or the other would slide through the snow
to the river where they usually bathed
and change a few things around
When one finally began to remind the other of herself
they got up. To support themselves
they took a job as death
and everyone who died agreed
that they looked perfect together

Private Lives
for M. E. H.

How long we live should only be measured
in the use of radio tubes
The nights at home when everything goes well
clarinet music and the soft red glow of the dial
outlining your shoulder is measure enough
of how we've come to need only one pillow
learned to walk protectively at the edge
of each other's mild nightmares

I believe I'll not get any older:
sitting across from you in someone's wintered-in house
both of us in thick, ugly sweaters
its good to think of going home to books
and small animals and such personal disarrangement
where the radio's in touch with polished pianos
and amber lights that only play and wonderfully,
mean nothing at all

One evening we'll have a room full of people
bent on 'accomplishing things'
when they've begun clinking glasses
and biting each other's fingers
lead them into our dark bedroom
softly aglow with humming tubes and say
this is the inside story
the light, the hum, the close private lives

Comfort me with your shoulders
given time, everything will be easy
I don't want to use my life
I'd rather pretend I'm slowly
dancing it away

In Music, in the Dreamer's Dance

This season I have made for you with my mind
to be free of a lifelong education in discipline
Stolen into my keeping I cannot let you be involved
with other lives or shared
by once seen faces
                  my love, remember no one

as you stand privately in the moon's shadow
Softly, I take off my kingly robes, remove
the ungraceful sandals
a thousand years younger stepping barefoot
off the dark pavillion where the last dancers perhaps
are drifting into sleep
the music will play all night
                  and phantoms will come to kiss you

these gardens I made deep with old dreams
insects for memory
thorns for time
Unafraid, you walk amidst my dreams, whispering
to creatures I bore in long nightmares
and they adore you, becoming tame and no longer ugly
tonight you shall pass untroubled
                  through my mind's terrors

finally alone, I recount to you the seasons of the mind
in moon, in music, in the dreamer's dance
curled in my arms you sigh openly
pulling me closer to you
as if you know which I will choose
when I consider selling slaves with the movements of your mouth
                  or letting them go free

When Worlds Collide Beneath Arches

It's become the type of life where love
has already formed the kind of arch
that precedes you into a room and sighs
but will not be questioned and gently resists
all attempts at dismantling
On my way to work in the morning if I see
your troubled face through wired glass in
old brick buildings I know enough
to spend the day away from the telephone and later,
not ask you what you did, how you felt
when I went away
If I simply position myself near a door and think
well, its possible not to
embrace you anymore
someone comes and invites us to a family hanging
and I am on my knees explaining
that it is not so much the lives of your brothers
or my brothers
but that somewhere in your small terrors
I am probably mentioned
I have probably caused all this with my stories
about becoming one with the loon
about reading your destiny in borrowed cards,
in the secrets of old women
Love has become the kind of arch
that can sleep with someone else's misery and whisper
so tenderly to passers-by
this is my deranged child that I bore
see how we comfort each other
see how she follows me and cannot weep
not knowing really who did this
whose unfinished jungle is tangled in her hands

when worlds collide
I see you wandering in the burnt-out landscape
wrapped in your blue mood and frightening dreams
Rising out of the rubble I will give you up
only to become a glowing eye
now floating just above your head
now resting wearily against your damaged spine

Invitation

The last time I accepted one
of these invitations it was
three weeks before I could stop

drawing frantic pictures of your stomach
Tell me, little warm body is this
one of those friends-of-the-trees parties or

shall I pay my rent again and start
designing legs, mouths, and
general disorder

The Dance Master Defeated by This Insane Love

The bad nights I couldn't love anybody and crawled
across the floor straining through too may lives
I lost something of myself to you
There were your frail dreams caught in the peril
of my terrible dreams to keep me
away from myself, to keep me
balanced between danger and creation
Return nothing to me; you have perhaps,
what I wanted you to have

I bring you into the mystery of insane love
that shadows me
I pour silver into your bones
and watch you shine
Shine on, scream, I bring you
into the mystery of my dark love
that guides your frail dreams through my terrible dreams
without harm
Leave yourself with me
I will distil a balance between safety
and this ceaseless, this desperate love

dark, I am the warring moon
pale, you are the drifting moon that dreams a war
to shatter space and illusion
I bring you into the mystery of my illusion
but such a gentle light is too kind an illusion
to drift, or shatter, or fear terrible dreams
instead

the dance master taps his baton and says
ready girls

and the girls do not dance, wandering off
to murmur
I never hurt you fool, I was
asleep

remember when you took my painful body into your arms
and broke open my veins to show
only a soft gold light within
and I said *walk off now with death*
I feel the mercy of the twice born
born in me
and you only fell asleep in my arms
and didn't give death a chance
and let me hold your shining, dancing heart

Will Someone Who is Not Guilty

Will someone who is not given to
vague feelings of terror and guilt please come over
and remove my telephone?
Suddenly, people with quavering voices have
taken to calling me at strange hours of the night
and asking for Angelica
I once did terrible things to a girl named
Angelica and I hate to think
what all this means

Evenings in the Sea

I feel such people making love behind old stairways
crooning wordless syllables to themselves
In burned out armories they lay themselves down
    in charred brick
rocking back and forth in arms that touch and linger
as much on one skin as on the other
On evenings born of a blue mood I feel them in the sea
turning the color of old suns as they
drift across the meridians,
men who cannot remember what a man is
and women, releasing fingernails and hair
turning forever back to a lover they do not
chastise or name
In the middle of the day I feel people disappearing quietly
in pairs, forgetting form and gender,
slipping deep into the sky
with whoever sat beside them on the train
or had the right time on the way to work
In my mind I am everyone,
needing you if only to have something of myself
Close your eyes and forget me,
tell me what you regret
and we will go on

Because I Will Never Love Another

Having loved you once
was in itself sufficient
so that although I was
too busy with your eyes (your hands)
to build you painted galleons
or hammers of gold
the rest of my life (ages and ages and ages)
I award, with great ceremony
in your honor

o time thy flesh and splendor

As in a Dream I Would Yet Remain

By counting newspapers piling up against
locked restaurant doors I never slept for weeks
keeping you from the river wind
I held your hair back from your eyes as you
slept against my shoulder, sometimes asking for your brother
from somewhere in a dream (did you dream of families,
of large beds?)

how much did you trust me
that even lost in these intricate american cities
you could so easily sleep in my arms
while I sat beside you in doorways, in the alleys
behind bars
guarding you against broken glass, against
the river winter

how much did you believe I would protect you
that you took money from off-duty policemen
and stole aspirin from crowded drugstores
for my shaking hands, my bleeding eyes

how much did you need me that you never questioned
what we would do
as homeless, drugged, we slept in silent american cities
eating nothing that contained protein or vitamins
or taste

Frances, even now I would remain with you
and rock you safely in your dreams

in every city I saw houses full of old women and
crippled St Bernards
and no one visited them
and all their lovers were dead

The Rest of Us End Up Incoherent

If I were possessed of a better moral character
I would not be lost in a boarded-up
industrial district at the end of Manhattan
with this small girl whose make-up
is running and a pocket full
(a bloodstream full) of illegal commodities

I guess some of us are born to be charming and
run gaily by the evening shore for
feminine deodorant commercials while the rest of us
end up poor and incoherent
babbling about drunken visions
and dying with people we don't know

13-100

PS
3562
.E67
A9

Lerman, Eleanor

Armed love.